Original title:
In the Shade of Sonnets

Copyright © 2025 Creative Arts Management OÜ
All rights reserved.

Author: Maxwell Donovan
ISBN HARDBACK: 978-1-80566-609-7
ISBN PAPERBACK: 978-1-80566-894-7

Fragments of Light in Lyrical Nooks

In corners bright, the shadows play,
A dancing cat joins the ballet.
The teapot whistles, loud and clear,
While socks and spoons engage in cheer.

A garden gnome with a silly grin,
Claims it's the best place to begin.
Butterflies argue who's best in flight,
While we sip tea, enjoying the sight.

The sun slips low, the colors swirl,
A worm in a hat does a tiny twirl.
With each new verse, the laughter grows,
As life unfolds in silly prose.

So grab a friend and share a rhyme,
In our oddball world, we've got the time.
Where puns sprout up like daisies bright,
And giggles linger, pure delight.

Dreams Entwined with Ink and Leaves

A squirrel dons a paper crown,
Declares he's king of this small town.
He hops on branches, grand and spry,
While poets drink from mugs nearby.

The ink flows freely, tales take flight,
As crickets chirp all through the night.
With leaves as pages, dreams unfold,
In whispers soft, their secrets told.

A turtle winks; he won't be late,
To join the fun, it's never fate.
With every word, we find our bliss,
In a world that sparkles with a twist.

So let's inscribe our laughter true,
In the soft glow of twilight's hue.
With ink and joy, we weave the seams,
In a land where everyone dreams.

The Poetry of Hidden Enclaves

Amidst the weeds, a secret lies,
Where daisies gossip, oh so wise.
A hedgehog hums a quirky tune,
While raindrops dance with the afternoon.

Behind the bushes, jokes are spun,
As patience fades, the laughter runs.
Each line a mystery, thick and sly,
With winks exchanged as we pass by.

In hidden nooks, where shadows meet,
We share our tales on trickster's street.
A toad recites, in croaks, delight,
While friends unite beneath the night.

So gather 'round, let stories flow,
In our enclave, the world's aglow.
With whimsical dreams and chuckles shared,
Let lyrics play, for none are snared.

Verses Hidden from the Sun

Beneath the ferns, a rabble rants,
A band of ants in silly pants.
With every line, their antics bloom,
As laughter echoes in the gloom.

The shadiest spots become their stage,
Where centipedes perform in rage.
Each verse a spark of crazed delight,
In a world where mischief takes flight.

A shadow weaves through lowly vines,
Tickling folks with playful lines.
With whispers soft, and grins so sly,
We tip our hats to passerby.

Let's pen the quirks that nature brings,
In secret spaces, where laughter clings.
As moonlight drapes, our giggles run,
In hidden verses, away from sun.

Chants Under the Arbor

Beneath the leaves, we dance and twirl,
A squirrel steals our snacks, oh what a curl!
The branches sway, a lullaby so sweet,
We laugh and sing with bare, happy feet.

The sun peeks through, a playful tease,
Tickling our noses, swaying with the breeze.
A butterfly lands, a silent comedian,
We clap and cheer, our forest's median.

Harmonizing with the Forest

Nobody told the trees to hum,
Yet here we are, unless them or come!
Mossy jokes stick like old dear friends,
Their laughter echoes, the fun never ends.

The owls hoot complaints, a feathery crowd,
While rabbits giggle, quite not too loud.
Harmonizing tunes with chirps of cheer,
The forest rocks on, pulling us near.

The Ode-Laden Breeze

Oh breezy whispers, what tales you weave,
With every gust, I can hardly believe!
A dandelion's wish floats by with glee,
As I trip on roots, then laugh at the tree.

The flowers gossip in colors bright,
Throwing snickers that dance in the light.
A bumblebee buzzes, tipsy and round,
While leaves clap their hands, such joy can be found.

Solitary Serenades

Alone, I sing to the chirping crew,
With critters as my fans, it's quite the view.
A raccoon rolls over, with laughter to share,
While shadows take part, no need for a chair.

The moss is my carpet, the sun is my stage,
In nature's grand play, I've entered the cage.
So I make a silly face, a wild charade,
For every chuckle is a memory made.

Muses in the Mist

The poet stumbles, quite a sight,
Chasing shadows in the night.
A muse appears with a wink,
Sipping coffee, starting to think.

Her laughter echoes, fills the air,
He scribbles fast, with a flair.
Words dance like leaves on a breeze,
Tickling thoughts with funny tease.

With rhymes that twist like a pretzel,
She shows him how to wrestle.
He chuckles, rolls with delight,
In quirky tales, they take flight.

So if you see them, don't be shy,
Join the laughter, give it a try.
For muses in the morning mist,
Are quite a giggle, I insist!

A Courtship of Couplet Trees

Two trees stand, side by side,
Flirting softly, full of pride.
Their branches twist, they sway and bow,
Sharing secrets, here and now.

The oak says, "You've grown so tall!"
The birch laughs, "But not so small!"
They rustle leaves, a whispered date,
Rooted deep in love's own fate.

They conjure dreams upon the breeze,
Jokes about squirrels, if you please.
With laughter ringing through the glen,
It's quite the courtship, now and then.

As seasons change, they laugh with glee,
Together weathering history.
In this forest green and wide,
The couplet trees laugh side by side.

Rhymes in Reverie

In a field of daisies wild,
A poet dreams, a happy child.
He spins tall tales of fluffy sheep,
Chasing clouds while giggling deep.

With rhymes that tickle like a breeze,
He crafts a world where nobody sees.
A frog recites, a snail applauds,
As butterflies cheer, in the oddest of squads.

He sways with joy, his pen in hand,
Writing treats that taste so grand.
With silly verses, puns in pairs,
He spreads laughter, floating through air.

So tiptoe softly, join the fun,
In rhymes where giggles never shun.
A reverie of silly glee,
Such joyful nonsense, come and see!

Tales from the Thicket

In the thicket, stories bloom,
With creatures chuckling, feel the room.
A raccoon jests, a fox with flair,
While rabbits giggle without a care.

They gather 'round a log so wide,
Sharing tales, with no need to hide.
A fable of a cat so sly,
Who thought he'd fly, but couldn't quite try.

The owl hoots, "What a sight to see!"
While the mouse ponders, should it be me?
With each punchline, the sun goes down,
A laughter fest in this leafy crown.

So if you wander through this glade,
Join their stories, don't be afraid.
For tales from thickets always flow,
With funny quirks, and laughs to grow!

Rhythms Caught in Gentle Breezes

A feather falls, I laugh and spin,
Caught in the dance, let the pranks begin.
A squirrel's chitter breaks the calm,
Stealing snacks like it's a charm.

With upside-down smiles, we sway with cheer,
Tickling the trees, it's the best time of year.
The sun winks shyly, clouds play peek,
Whispering secrets while we sneak a treat.

Chasing shadows, we tumble and roll,
The breeze carries laughter, tickling our soul.
So come join the fun, there's mischief in air,
As we spin through the day, light as a prayer.

Every giggle wraps us, a cozy cocoon,
In this laughter waltz, we'll be back soon.
So let's make some noise, till evening's reply,
As giggles and breezes swoosh by and fly.

The Silent Embrace of Couplets

Two peas in a pod, we joke and tease,
Like socks with a hole, oh what a breeze!
Your camera flashes, the pose is absurd,
Caught mid-laugh, it's the best kind of nerd.

Drawing hearts with crayons, we color outside,
While giggling at dreams that we both tried to hide.
Each couplet a giggle, stitched with delight,
In this wacky tale, our laughter takes flight.

Like pancakes flipped high, we dance on the floor,
With syrupy puns, then we just want more.
Countdown to mischief, with friend in tow,
In playful rhythms, we're free to just flow.

So hold tight to jests, let the wild times unfold,
For in every line, our saga is told.
With jokes as our compass, we venture through night,
Side by side in this whimsical flight.

Twilight Thoughts on Petaled Pages

As twilight whispers, petals start to dance,
We chase down the light, oh what a chance!
With thoughts that tickle, they spin and sway,
Twilight's soft giggles steal worries away.

Each page a canvas, with colors so bright,
We paint silly stories in warm fading light.
With butterflies chuckling, we linger too long,
Creating a chorus, our own silly song.

Under the stars, we craft rhymes so sweet,
With every word tumbles a laugh or a tweet.
So here in this twilight, the jokes softly fly,
As petals giggle back, in a glancing goodbye.

So let's snap a snapshot, this giggle-filled night,
In journals of joy, where dreams take flight.
With laughter like lanterns, we'll twirl and we'll play,
In petaled pages, where folly holds sway.

Melodies Woven in Dappled Light

Under a tree, where shadows play,
We gather our laughter, in sunlight's array.
With dappled rays as our giggle guide,
Each note bursts forth, like a giddy tide.

Hidden in laughter, we jingle and jive,
While ants march past, ten thousand alive!
Our serenade swells, a quirky delight,
As melodies dance in the warm, golden light.

We spin silly tales, under branches so high,
Where owls roll their eyes and the blue jays fly.
With every chorus, we tickle the breeze,
This symphony of jest whispers sweetly through trees.

So join in the fun, let the worlds collide,
In the gentle embrace where laughter resides.
With melodies woven in dappled light,
Let the day drift away, into starry night.

Poesy at Dusk

A squirrel with a hat, oh what a sight,
Doing a dance, laughing at night.
A moonlit cheese platter, a toast to the breeze,
Whispers of rhymes under swaying trees.

The fireflies giggle, they flash and they twirl,
As verses take flight, a poetic swirl.
With every soft flicker, new jokes to unfold,
In twilight's embrace, hilarities told.

Echoes Beneath the Canopy

Beneath leafy arches, the crickets conspire,
Each chirp a punchline, a lyrical fire.
The owls in their wisdom, roll eyes to the stars,
As raccoons exchange puns, while munching on jars.

A lost sock's own journey, now crafted in verse,
It traveled quite far, like the world in reverse!
With laughter all around, even shadows do grin,
As the night giggles softly, inviting us in.

The Melancholy of Metaphors

Oh, the sad little metaphor, longing for rhyme,
It wanders the hills, lost in silly time.
A fish out of water, wearing a frown,
With dreams of being king, of a seashell crown.

Yet humor prevails, as the clouds drift away,
A simile's smile brightens up the gray.
Each line a chuckle, every stanza a jest,
For laughter is cosmic, and life's just a fest.

A Grotto of Starlit Words

In a grotto of whispers, the galaxies joke,
With comets that tease, and moonbeams that poke.
A star with a quip, 'I shine for the fun!'
While comical constellations dance on the run.

The cosmos chuckles, as comets play tag,
While nebulae giggle, in shimmering swag.
A tapestry woven of mirth and of glee,
In this witty expanse, we just want to be.

A Tapestry of Trees

Under a leafy roof, we hide,
Squirrels peek out, eyes open wide.
One drops a nut, it hits my head,
I laugh and wonder, 'who's really fed?'

The branches sway, a gentle tease,
Whispers of jokes carried by the breeze.
A crow caws out, a punchline clear,
I toss him breadcrumbs, he brings good cheer.

Sunshine winks through a leafy curtain,
A worm complains, 'This feels certain.'
He wriggles out, with sass and pride,
In this green theater, no need to hide.

We dance with shadows, a merry sight,
Sunflowers grin, oh what delight!
With every giggle, the world feels bright,
In this leafy laughter, everything's right.

Metrical Murmurs

A frog croaks rhymes by the pond,
With leaps and bounds, of him I'm fond.
His poetic skills are quite profound,
In every splash, new verses found.

The dragonflies swirl, on mini quests,
Playing tag, they put me to the test.
Their zipping lines, a funny sight,
They dip and dive, much to my delight.

A turtle hums in a slow parade,
He may be slow, but he's never swayed.
With every note, he takes a break,
His music floats like a froggy lake.

Amidst the reeds, a laughter fest,
Nature's rhymes put me to rest.
In this weird world of rhyme and glee,
Every croak and chirp is poetry!

Silhouetted Ballads

In twilight's glow, shadows dance,
A cat sings low, as if by chance.
He struts along, a rock star's flare,
With every yowl, he claims the air.

The fireflies blink, a twinkling show,
They mock the stars, with lights that flow.
A clumsy moth flops to the ground,
In this concert of bugs, joy abounds.

The owls hoot a deep-toned song,
While crickets chirp, they can't go wrong.
Together they weave a nightly jest,
In nature's chime, we find our rest.

With silhouettes casting shadows tall,
The moon joins in, a soft curtain call.
We giggle and sway in this grand parade,
A silly ballad where our dreams are made.

Twilight's Vocal Canvas

At dusk's embrace, the world turns sweet,
Rabbits hop about, on little feet.
They dance in circles, a vibrant spree,
With every twitch, they charm the trees.

An old owl grumbles, 'It's just too bright!'
While fireflies wink, teasing the night.
A wandering breeze sings a gentle tune,
As stars peek out, one by one, soon.

A hedgehog rolls, in a furry ball,
He giggles softly, never feels small.
In this quirky scene, joy takes flight,
Nature's chorus, alive with delight.

As twilight colors the evening sky,
Laughter echoes, no need to be shy.
In this canvas of whimsy, we play,
Crafting memories in a brilliant array.

The Veiled Quill

A quill that snickers, takes its stance,
With ink that dances, joins the prance.
It scribbles tales of cats in hats,
And feisty mice that duel with bats.

Each word it writes, a comical jest,
About a bird that fails its nest.
It giggles softly, tickles the reed,
Bringing to life a wild-eyed steed.

Inking up laughter, creating delight,
Turning mundane to pure, sheer height.
The quill, it knows the funny bone,
With each stroke, the humor's shown.

So laugh, my friend, with every line,
For wit and humor together shine.
In every tale, hilarity built,
Dance with the quill, embrace the silt.

Shadows and Silhouettes of Stanza

Shadows whisper, a giggle or two,
As stanzas skip, and jump askew.
Like shadows of trees that twiddle and sway,
They crack jokes in a quirky ballet.

Each line a silhouette, prancing with glee,
Riddles of rhymes, in playful decree.
The punchline lurking, just out of sight,
Waiting for laughter to take its flight.

These shadows, they dart, with mischief in mind,
Chasing the sun, leaving woes behind.
In the dance of verse, they twist and they twirl,
Crafting a tale where giggles unfurl.

So join in the frolic, let laughter blend,
For in shadows of lines, the fun has no end.
With each little twinkle, life's brighter, you see,
In silhouettes dressed, in pure jubilee.

Petals of Lyrical Lore

Petals are flinging, a colorful mess,
Each verse a giggle, no chance to stress.
Whispers of flowers, gossiping sweet,
About a bee with two left feet.

The garden is thriving, with rhymes in bloom,
Tall tales of insects that curtsy and swoon.
A daffodil snickers at the old oak tree,
Who claims he's the wisest, oh, can't you see?

Under beams of sunshine, laughter takes flight,
Petals are bouncing, such a curious sight.
In the floral embrace, humor thrives bold,
With every story of old age retold.

So wander the garden, where fun leads the way,
With petals and verses in sunny array.
In lyrical lore, joy's hiding in plain sight,
Join in the jesting, everything feels right.

The Whispering Grove of Poetry

In the grove where verses play hide and seek,
Whispers of humor, soft, yet unique.
Trees chuckle gently, leaves sway in cheer,
As owls crack jokes, "What's with this sphere?"

The breeze carries laughter, tickles your neck,
While squirrels debate, "Is this rhyme, or a wreck?"
A rabbit recites its own silly creed,
"Why do we hop? For fun, indeed!"

In this quiet haven, words flutter and flight,
Where poetry's spirit ignites the night.
Giggles resound, like echoes of jest,
In the whispering grove, let humor take rest.

So prance through the stanzas, let giggles arise,
In the grove of laughter, be ready for surprise.
With each playful whisper, joy's ever near,
Embrace the absurd, let go of the fear.

Whispers Beneath the Canopy

Under the leaves, a squirrel prances,
Chasing its dreams, while nature glances.
A rhyme tumbles down with giggles and glee,
All while a bee takes a sip of my tea.

A professor once said, 'Life's like a rhyme,'
I chuckled and whispered, 'A waste of good time!'
For under this shade, where nonsense is king,
We dance with the leaves and let laughter take wing.

Echoes of Verse in Twilight

The moon whispers jokes to the stars overheard,
While owls hoot punchlines, oh how they'd concur!
Frivolous critters come out for the laughs,
They hold poetry slams in groups of blue giraffes.

A cat in a top hat juggles big fish,
While frogs play the drums, oh what a wild wish!
It's a spectacle here, beneath starry glows,
Where laughter ignites, and the funny bone grows.

Secrets in the Garden of Rhymes

In the garden where daisies tell tales of the past,
The weeds giggle softly, their jokes unsurpassed.
A tulip mocks roses, and lilies join in,
They laugh at their thorns, 'Who needs such a grin?'

A hedgehog recites in a voice slightly croaky,
While ladybugs buzz like, 'Life's one big hokey!'
With punchlines blooming, it's a vibrant display,
In sundrenched chaos, all woes melt away.

Beneath the Boughs of Stanza

A hammock's a throne for the king of the jest,
As I dish out puns, feel the humor manifest.
The breeze chips in, making everything light,
While crickets join in with their chirpy delight.

The sky gets a chuckle from clouds on parade,
As shadows play pranks that the sun's not afraid.
In this wordy retreat, where silliness reigns,
We trade all our worries for giggles and gains.

Harmonies of Hushed Horizons

Under a sky so bright and clear,
The birds sing songs we love to hear.
A squirrel danced with a wobbly tail,
While I sat down, sipping my ale.

A butterfly stole my sandwich slice,
I guess it thought it looked so nice.
In the chaos of crumbs and cheer,
Nature's laughter drew me near.

The trees giggled as leaves did sway,
Whispering secrets about the day.
I lost my hat to a cheeky crow,
Who wore it proudly, stealing the show.

With each gust of wind, life's a jest,
In this haven, I'll take a rest.
As tickled toes meet the grass below,
Joy blooms bright in every flow.

The Calm Between the Lines

With every page, the plot does twist,
Yet bits of chaos make me laugh and tryst.
Where characters trip and fall in glee,
Finding love 'neath the old oak tree.

A villain sneezes, oh what a sight,
The hero winks, 'This'll be alright.'
A talking cat steals the show with flair,
Chasing shadows without a care.

In the margins, doodles come to life,
A knight on a dragon, avoiding strife.
Each stanza bursts with playful quirks,
As the mundane breaks with funny perks.

The calm between lines is never bland,
Where imagination takes a stand.
A world unfolds, ludicrous yet grand,
All penned down by a playful hand.

Intimacies of Ink and Earth

With ink spills and coffee stains galore,
Adventures bloom as I scribble more.
An ant's opinion? Too sweet to ignore,
As he nods and offers life's encore.

The ink pot's a fountain, it laughs and plays,
Washing the dullness of long, rainy days.
A leaf turns up with a lettered grin,
Whispering tales from where it's been.

Crickets chirp poems under the moon,
In harmony with nature's tune.
A rock claps quietly, holding court,
Sharing secrets in a playful sort.

Ink and earth twirl in a silly dance,
Turning words into a comical chance.
In their embrace, imagination's worth,
Grows wild and free, like a sprightly mirth.

Versed Journeys in Quiet Groves

In quiet groves, where whispers soar,
Adventure waits behind every door.
A mischievous raccoon steals my snack,
While I ponder if he'll give it back.

The trees tell stories with their tangled limbs,
Of brave little worms and twiggy whims.
Each breeze brings laughter, light as a feather,
As flowers gossip about gloomy weather.

Underneath bramble, a playful scene,
An iguana struts, flipping through green.
He strikes a pose, so bold, so grand,
While I burst out laughing — oh, what a stand!

So in this grove of silly delights,
We carve our names into starry nights.
Where nature's comedy comes and goes,
I find my joy in the tales she sows.

Shadows of Rhyme

In the park, a squirrel danced,
Twisting limbs, the critter pranced.
An old man laughed, his hat flew high,
As he tried to catch it, oh my, oh my!

Beneath the trees, a picnic spread,
But ants conspired to steal their bread.
With funny faces and silly sounds,
Chaos erupted, joy abounds!

A dog named Max wore silly shades,
Chasing shadows in playful raids.
While laughter echoed in the grass,
Life's simple joys made moments last.

So let us dance beneath the sky,
With rhymes and laughs, oh, let us fly!
For in this park of quirky charms,
We find the magic in each other's arms.

Crescendos Beneath Canopies

Under branches, shadows groove,
A choir of birds begins to move.
Chirps and whistles, out of key,
Like a concert gone topsy-turvy!

A frog on a lily, dressed to impress,
Croaked his solo, causing a mess.
While flowers giggled, swaying low,
With pollen flying, a jaunty show.

The sun peeked down, with a winking face,
As butterflies joined the silly race.
Around and around, in dizzying spins,
Nature's folly, where giggle begins!

So here we sit beneath the bow,
With laughter rippling, take a bow!
For crescendos rise in playful delight,
Creating magic from day into night.

The Garden of Stanzas

In a garden where words bloom bright,
A daisy sneezed with all its might.
Pollen flew and petals soared,
While bees buzzed in laughter, adored.

A rose tried to rhyme with a thistle,
But ended up in a stubborn bristle.
"Oh my," it mused, "that's not quite right,
Maybe I'll stick to that bumblebee flight!"

Vegetables joined in a whimsical line,
Carrots tap-danced, feeling so fine.
While cabbage heads rolled in fits of glee,
Creating a ballet for all to see!

The soil laughed, a comical mess,
With roots intertwining in sheer success.
Together they weave a tale of fun,
In this garden of stanzas, everyone's won!

Echoes of Timeless Lines

With a giggle, the echoes play,
Whispering secrets of yesterday.
A lost sock, a shoe on a tree,
What mysteries lie where we can't see?

The wind carried tales of clumsy falls,
As leaves danced wildly, bouncing off walls.
Laughter ricocheted through the air,
Tickling the sun with the softest care.

Amidst the echoes, a wise old crow,
Cracked a riddle, putting on a show.
As we pondered, we saw the time fly,
With joy and humor, we laughed 'til we cried!

In these rhythmic echoes, we find our place,
Transcending troubles with a silly face.
For even in chaos, laughter aligns,
Creating memories in timeless lines.

Verses in Twilight

Under the sky, a frog sings loud,
Wearing a crown, feeling so proud.
He dances on lily pads so grand,
Claiming himself the king of the land.

Fireflies twinkle, a shimmering show,
While crickets chirp to the rhythm below.
A turtle cheers from the muddy edge,
Waving a leaf like a tiny pledge.

Bats swoop by, in their nightly flight,
Mistaking a hat for a tasty bite.
Laughter erupts from the buzzing bees,
As they tickle the nose of a dancing tree.

Stars peek out, joining the fun,
With jokes about the moon and how it's spun.
The night rolls on, a whimsical spree,
In the twilight glow, so wild and free.

Serenades Among the Leaves

A squirrel recites a comedic tale,
Of acorns lost and a brave dog's wail.
He pauses to snicker at the trees,
Who shake their branches in a playful breeze.

The wind hums softly, a mischievous tune,
While flowers blush beneath the bold moon.
A whispering vine shares puns by the root,
As nearby gnomes giggle, wearing strange boots.

Rabbits plan parties, carrots in hand,
With disco lights made from a broken strand.
They bounce around, creating a scene,
With a boisterous beat; it's quite the routine!

Amidst all the laughter, a wise owl sighs,
"Why do we party? Well, why not try?"
And so the night drifts, filled with delight,
As critters unite in pure joy and light.

The Canopy of Cadence

Under ripe branches, a goat grins wide,
Juggling some fruit, a curious ride.
He slips on a banana, oh what a fall!
The forest erupts; oh, did you see that wall?

Bees in formation dance to the beat,
As a hedgehog joins in, tapping his feet.
The sun bows down, casting shadows of fun,
Mischief unfolds, 'till the day is done.

Whispers of berries in a playful chat,
As gnomes gather 'round, all wearing a hat.
"Oh, here comes a worm with jokes so dry!"
The giggles resound as the clouds float by.

The trees clap their branches in glee at the sight,
While squirrels crack jokes till the stars are in sight.
And in the ruckus, life finds its way,
In a canopy of cadence, we dance and sway.

Moonlight Over Metrical Paths

Under the moon, a snail moves slow,
With dreams of races, he puts on a show.
His friends all chuckle, cheering the plight,
As they wait for the dawn to end the night.

A clock ticks loudly, but no one cares,
The fireflies gather for silly dares.
"Shall we glow brighter or turn off our lights?"
They burst out laughing as the air ignites.

A cat floats by on a cloud of cream,
Chasing a shadow, lost in the dream.
With whiskers wiggling, she sways so free,
In the moonlight comedy, oh how it be!

Stars roll their eyes, enjoying the hum,
As the laughter swells, it becomes a drum.
The night remains vibrant with whimsy, oh dear,
As we dance on the paths, a celebration cheer!

Mysteries Wrapped in Metaphor

A pickle danced beneath the moon,
Its briney jig made all of us swoon.
In socks that clashed with every hue,
We laughed till dawn, the night just flew.

The cat wore glasses, quite absurd,
While plotting schemes that were unheard.
He sipped his tea with utmost grace,
And left us baffled, a puzzled face.

A pizza slice said, "I need friends!"
As pepperoni rolled, the laughter bends.
With every giggle, secrets arise,
In silent whispers and playful sighs.

So let us toast to tales unspun,
Of quirky dances and morning sun.
Life's little mysteries, wrapped so tight,
Bring endless joy, from dusk till light.

Chronicles of the Quiet Evening

A squirrel skated on the fence,
Wearing a hat, what common sense!
With acorns stacked in high demand,
He's the king of this quiet land.

The moonlight giggled, casting glee,
As shadows danced beside the tree.
With whispers soft like cotton candy,
We pondered fate with thoughts so dandy.

Birds in tuxedos held a soirée,
Chirping sonnets in perfect ballet.
With crickets in tuxes, bowing low,
They made the night a fabulous show.

In this quaint space, laughter appears,
With tales of whimsy to soothe our fears.
Chronicles spin from mundane to grand,
In this quiet evening, the fun is unplanned.

Lifting the Veil of Dappled Darkness

A chocolate frog sat on a log,
Debating with a sleepy dog.
They spoke of dreams and buttered toast,
In dappled darkness, wild to boast.

A moonbeam peeked through leafy lace,
Tickling shadows, a playful chase.
With giggles rising in the night,
They juggled stars—a comical sight.

The gnomes conspired with pots of gold,
Sharing tales that never grow old.
With every sparkle, a wink, a jest,
In the veil's embrace, we found our rest.

So come, dear friends, join this parade,
Of whimsical thoughts that never fade.
In depths of night, let laughter flow,
As wonders bloom in the moon's soft glow.

Whispers of Verses

A bubble floated, bold and round,
It whispered secrets without a sound.
While giggling ducks took to the stream,
They quacked in rhythm, living the dream.

With every tickle from the breeze,
The flowers nodded with such ease.
As butterflies wore costumes bright,
They danced and twirled, what a sight!

A sandwich sang a silly tune,
Under the watchful eye of the moon.
With laughter wrapping all around,
These whispered verses in joy abound.

So let the stories freely blend,
Of pickles, bubbles, delight we send.
In every corner, a chuckle resides,
In the magic of words, where fun abides.

Harmonies of Hidden Words

A letter fell, it took a dive,
It swam away, oh how it jives!
A vowel danced with a cheeky grin,
While consonants said, 'Let's begin!'

In paper boats, they sailed the ink,
Moored at a thought, or so they think.
Each word a buddy, each sentence a crew,
They laugh at me, and you laugh too!

With puns afloat, they start to play,
"Is that a real word?" you hear them say.
A thesaurus joins, tries to fit in,
Says, "Hey, that's clever!" with a wink and spin.

So when you write, just let it flow,
Let nonsense reign, let laughter grow.
For words are silly, they twist and twirl,
Creating humor, in this wild world!

The Quietude of Quatrains

Four lines stand quiet, balmy mess,
Their secret giggles, they try to confess.
A rhyme with a wig, a beat that's absurd,
Whispers of laughter, it's quite unheard.

In corners they plot, oh what a sight!
A stanza in pajamas, looking just right.
With rhymes in the fridge, and meter on a spree,
They toast to the mischief, just wait and see!

"Who's taking the lead?" says a line with a frown,
As puns from the back row start throwing it down.
A quatrain, it beckons, "Come dance with me!"
As laughter erupts, like popcorn, you see.

From whispers to screams, in the glow of the night,
They prance and they hop, what a humorous sight!
So gather your quatrains, let's all have a blast,
In the quirkiest rhyme, let bright moments last!

Starlit Stanzas

Beneath the stars, a stanza sings,
Chasing the moon with whimsical wings.
Each syllable floats, a spark in the sky,
Where laughter meets rhymes, oh my oh my!

The commas are crickets, the periods mice,
A semicolon does a dance, oh how nice!
They twirl through the air, with glee in their way,
As the laughter spills out at the end of the day.

A verse with a smile, a punchline on cue,
The laughter erupts, like morning dew.
As starlit ideas begin to compare,
One shouts in delight, "Is that really fair?"

So catch the giggles, let stanzas collide,
In the warmth of the night, let humor be tried.
For with each jolly line, a star gets its shine,
And in this vast universe, we all intertwine!

Rhythms Cradled in Green

In leafy nooks, the rhythms play,
A funny tune, as bright as day.
The grass chuckles, the branches sway,
As rhymes emerge in a comical ballet.

A frog finds a beat, a cricket hums low,
The flowers all chuckle, don't you know?
With petals as partners, they dance in delight,
As verses tumble out into the twilight.

The bushes whisper secrets, a pun or two,
As laughter rings loud, like morning dew.
With nature's own chorus, a jolly refrain,
They serenade the silence, breaking the chain.

So stroll through the green, let the rhythms take flight,
With laughter and joy, make the world feel bright.
For every small whisper, in foliage keen,
Is humor wrapped up in the shades of green!

Secrets of Solitude in Stanza

When squirrels plot a heist anew,
They giggle beneath the branches too.
Whispers shared with playful glee,
Nature's secrets, just you and me.

A bird on a branch sings a tune,
Dodging raindrops, it's quite the boon.
Trees eavesdrop with rustling leaves,
While ants march on, tucked in their sleeves.

Breezes tease with soft little pranks,
Nudging me while I write at the banks.
Scribbling my thoughts on crinkled bark,
I can't resist leaving my mark.

With each flutter, the fun never ends,
In this woodland world, laughter transcends.
Secrets shared in chuckles and sighs,
Who knew solitude could be such a surprise?

Moonlit Melodies on Leafy Pages

A frog croaked out a loud serenade,
While fireflies twinkled, unafraid.
Under the moon, giggles ignite,
Nature's stage is a curious sight.

A raccoon wearing a mask of night,
Dances with raciness, a comical sight.
Branches sway to the beat of his jig,
While the crickets cheer, doing a twig.

Scribbles of laughter shade the bright stars,
Creativity flows, smashing old bars.
In moments like these, dreams dance and blend,
While the night tells stories without an end.

Each leaf a page, each breeze a song,
Wrapping us in laughter all night long.
Moonlit melodies, oh what a blast,
Every beat and chuckle, forever to last.

The Heartbeat of Haikus Under Canopies

Beneath the greenery, whispers abound,
Chirps of the creatures all around.
With syllables dancing like butterflies,
Nature's poems, a grand surprise.

A warbler's note, a laugh from the leaves,
Playing tag with an ant that weaves.
In haiku form, they tell their tales,
Of flight and fun as the wind exhales.

Shade pools where shadows play peek-a-boo,
Sunbeams bounce 'round, giving a view.
Jokes of the forest are lightly found,
As laughter and rhythm solidly sound.

So gather your wits and listen in close,
To the giggles of leaves—they're charming as prose.
Through every heartbeat, the forest is wise,
In the realm of haikus, it's laughter that flies.

The Lure of Shadows and Sound

In twilight's embrace, shadows conspire,
Rustling secrets, feeding desire.
The echoing chuckles of light-footed deer,
Draw us nearer, whispering cheer.

Crickets play symphonies, wild and sweet,
While toads in the choir find their beat.
The branches sway, keeping time,
A nighttime dance, oh so sublime!

Chasing away worries, shadows grow bold,
Under their cloak, stories unfold.
Beneath the laughter of moonlit sound,
In nature's arms, peace we have found.

Lured by the whispers, come take a chance,
Join in the rhythm, share in the dance.
In this playful quiet, magic abounds,
We find joy in the melody of sounds.

Echoing in the Embrace of Trees

Under branches wide and low,
A squirrel dances to and fro.
Whispers giggle through the leaves,
As mischief tales the forest weaves.

A rabbit dons a top hat tight,
Declaring it a fine delight.
He tips it with a furry paw,
While birds break out in loud guffaws.

The leaves clap hands, they cheer and sway,
At every joke the trees would say.
Roots chuckle deep, they know the score,
As winds blow puns from door to door.

In this wood, laughter takes its flight,
As trees weave humor through the night.
So leave your worries, take a seat,
Join the woodland fun, oh what a treat!

The Sylvan Muse

A pine made jokes about a fir,
Said, "You're so sharp, you could concur!"
The crow was cackling up above,
Lending a laugh, a gift of love.

Mushrooms winked with painted grins,
As little ants planned playful sins.
They marched in line, a comical sight,
While frogs croaked tunes, oh pure delight!

The brook chimed in with bubbling glee,
Said, "I'm the best at melody!"
The stones just chuckled, rough and round,
In this wild, whimsical playground.

In shadows thick where stories grow,
Each leaf holds secrets, they surely know.
Nature's jest brings joy to roam,
In this comedy, we'll make our home!

Rhymes Beneath the Stars

At night, the moon pulls funny pranks,
It hides behind the clouds in flanks.
"Catch me if you can!" it beams,
As laughter dances in our dreams.

The stars are giggling, bright and bold,
They sprinkle joy like stories told.
A comet whizzes, shouts, "I'm fast!"
While planets joke about the past.

The nightingale flirts with the breeze,
Sings tunes that put you at your ease.
While owls hoot wisdom with a twist,
Their sage advice we can't resist.

Beneath this tapestry of light,
The universe crafts pure delight.
In every twinkle lies a jest,
A cosmic laugh, we are so blessed!

Shadows of Unwritten Legends

In the corners where shadows play,
Old legends whisper, come what may.
They chuckle low with tales of yore,
Of knights who tripped through castle doors.

Witches on brooms with hats askew,
Conjured potions that just went 'poof!'
Their cauldron bubbles, a silly stew,
As goblins plot their next big coup.

A dragon snores, a beast so grand,
Dreaming of gold and ice cream stands.
With every roar, the woods just giggle,
As tales unfold, they twist and wiggle.

So if you wander through the glades,
Join in the fun these legends made.
With every step and every sigh,
Laughter echoes, reaching high!

Ode to the Forgotten Lines

Oh, how the verses like to play,
They giggle and jump in a silly way!
With words that stumble and trip so fine,
Hidden in laughter, a forgotten line.

The rhymes are schemers, oh what a team,
They dance around like they're lost in a dream.
Puns and jests tickle the page,
A comedic quip from the poet's stage.

As stanzas wander, they trip on their feet,
A limerick twist makes it all quite a feat.
Banter and jest in this playful fray,
Who knew the lines could be so gay!

So raise up your pens, let the laughter ignite,
For with every chuckle, the words take flight.
Lost in the joy of this funny parade,
Ode to the lines, where the fun is made!

Serene Sonatas of Nature

In the forest's heart where the squirrels reside,
Nature hums sonatas, a whimsical guide.
The trees sway gently, with laughter they bend,
Singing soft melodies that never do end.

Birds chirp in harmony, a witty refrain,
While crickets join in with a comical gain.
A breeze blows through, tickling a leaf,
Nature's orchestra plays without grief.

With each rustle and whisper, a joke's in the air,
The flowers burst forth, in colorful flair.
Sunlight winks down, a mischievous sprite,
In serene sonatas that feel just so right.

Oh, joy in the melody, bright and alive,
Every sweet note makes the heart take a dive.
Thus dance with the flora, let laughter abound,
In nature's antics, pure joy can be found!

Verses in the Wilderness

Amidst the tall grass where the wild things play,
The verses run wild, in their own zany way.
With squirrels as muse, and a chipmunk's cheer,
Laughter erupts in this wilderness sphere.

The echoes of humor bounce off the trees,
While bees take a sip of the sweetest of teas.
The brook chuckles softly, a gurgling sound,
While poets meander where nonsense is found.

Those lines in the wild just can't sit quite still,
Tumbling down slopes with exuberant thrill.
With every word spun, a giggle takes flight,
Verses in jest, what a wonderful sight!

So venture forth, let your spirit unwind,
In the wilderness where humor you'll find.
Join the dance of the quips, let the laughter flow,
In wild, funny verses, let your joy grow!

The Secret Garden of Words

Tucked away in a nook where the oddball thoughts bloom,

Lives a garden of words in forgetfulness' room.
The petals are riddles, the thorns wrapped in laughs,
A secret so sweet, that it brightens the paths.

Words whisper softly like butterflies flit,
With puns taking flight, they seem to be writ.
In the soil of humor where dreams intertwine,
A riot of laughter and clever design.

Chickens in aprons will serve you a dish,
Of giggles and grins, it's a fanciful wish.
The blooms of absurdity sprout in delight,
In the secret garden, hilarity's right!

So wander through pages, let joy be your guide,
In the garden of whimsy, you'll never need hide.
With each stroke of your pen, let hilarity grow,
In this hidden retreat, let the chuckles bestow!

Lullabies of Luminous Lines

A hamster on a wheel, oh so spry,
He dreams of cheese, bacon, and pie.
With each little spin, he gives it a whirl,
In a world where kites are made of pearl.

A cat sings opera from the shelf,
While dogs tap dance all by themselves.
With hats on their heads, they form a band,
Singing of socks lost in the sand.

The goldfish plays piano, quite sublime,
While crickets keep rhythm all the time.
And owls in tuxedos, looking so dapper,
Throw a tea party that makes all hearts flapper.

So if you hear laughter from afar,
It's just the pets and their dancing char.
To lullabies that wriggle and rhyme,
Making us giggle, oh what a time!

Shadows Cradled in Meter

A frog in a tux, he croaks out a tune,
Dancing with fireflies beneath the moon.
His voice a croon, so charming, so bright,
To woo all the ladies, what a wild night!

The fish wear bowties, bold and grand,
As they float together, hand in hand.
With bubbles of laughter just floating by,
They swim through dreams that tickle and fly.

A mouse with a hat spins tales with glee,
Of cheese-filled castles and a grand jubilee.
But watch out for cats with their sneaky plans,
Who might join the dance, in their furry bands.

So gather 'round, join the merry parade,
In this wacky world where fun is made.
With shadows that twist, and laughter that sings,
Life's laced with the charm that silliness brings.

Reveries of the Moonlit Quatrain

A dragon eats cake, with frosting so thick,
He dreams of fairytales, prancing, and tricks.
Each slice goes missing, as quick as a flash,
Causing such giggles, a sweet, silly smash.

A raccoon in sandals, so quirky, so neat,
Sells lemonade, but it's fruit with a beat.
He juggles the cups while balancing right,
With a wink and a smile, he's a star of the night!

A unicorn sneezes, rainbow confetti,
Sprinkles the crowd, turning all nice and petty.
While elves on the sidelines, take a quick bow,
Spreading pure cheer with a magical wow!

So let the stories unfold as we read,
With laughter and joy, our hearts they will feed.
In whimsical realms, let our dreams take flight,
In moonlit quatrains, oh what a delight!

Where the Words Find Rest

Where socks disappear, that's where I'll go,
A land of lost things, all cozy and slow.
Here mismatched pairs throw a sock puppet show,
While lint bunnies twirl, putting on a glow.

A book with no cover, it whispers to me,
Of stories untold, surrounded by glee.
Pages filled with giggles, words sticking like glue,
Inviting the mice to join in the view.

Two apples debate about who is the best,
While a potato carries out a playful jest.
They roll on the floor, in a comical race,
Creating a whirlwind of colorful space.

So gather the words, let them dance on your tongue,
With laughter intertwined, life's song to be sung.
In the land of lost things, let's sit and invest,
For here all our whims, they truly can rest.

Gently Falling Words

Words drop like leaves,
They dance in the air,
Tickling my thoughts,
With laughter to share.

A phrase swings by,
Like a squirrel so spry,
Chasing around,
As the puns fly high.

Jokes hidden in rhymes,
Under branches they hide,
Whispers of chuckles,
Where gags coincide.

In this playful breeze,
Where the goofy reside,
I gather the fun,
And take it for a ride.

The Secret Life of Stanzas

Stanzas lay awake,
Plotting in their night,
With jokes up their sleeves,
And puns that take flight.

They giggle all night,
As the metaphors pout,
Turning prose into jokes,
That make us laugh out.

Each line takes a stroll,
With rhythm and cheer,
Sketching silly tales,
For all who come near.

Oh, the secret lives,
Behind every quill,
Witty whispers abound,
In the silence, they thrill.

Melodies at Play in the Foliage

Notes flutter like birds,
On branches they cling,
Bouncing off laughter,
With each joyous fling.

Syllables twist round,
Like vines in the sun,
Creating a chorus,
That's frolicsome fun.

Rhythms hum sweetly,
In the foliage bright,
While giggles cascade,
Like twinkling starlight.

Tunes sprout from the ground,
In this playful spree,
Melodies twirl high,
Like leaves from a tree.

The Whispering Wordwood

In the Wordwood grove,
Chatter fills the air,
Each phrase rustles soft,
With stories to share.

Echoes of laughter,
Bounce from tree to tree,
A pun-tastic parade,
For all hearts to see.

The bark whispers tales,
Of words gone astray,
Sending chuckles round,
In the light of day.

So gather your thoughts,
In this woodland of glee,
Where each little phrase,
Brings smiles endlessly.

Serenades of the Subtle Shade

Sipping tea while squirrels dance,
A cheeky chipmunk takes a chance.
It steals my sandwich, oh the shame,
I guess I'll have to share the blame.

The sunlight flickers, playfully,
A rabbit jumps, oh can't you see?
He winks at me, quite full of glee,
As if to say, 'Come join the spree!'

A butterfly flirts, in polka dots,
While I sit here in tangled knots.
They laugh as I trip on a shoe,
Perhaps the trees will help me too.

Nature's comic stage is set,
With every creature, a duet.
We all make blunders, yes, it's true,
But in this shade, we'll laugh anew.

Respite in the Arms of Lyricism

A melody hums, like bees at play,
While poets nap the afternoon away.
Their rhymes are silly, their rhythms askew,
Yet all around, the laughter grew.

They argue lines, with bumbled grace,
A sonnet's structure, a wild chase.
One drops his pen, and oh what fun,
It rolls away—let's all just run!

A duo sings, off-key and bold,
Twirling around like they're uncontrolled.
With every note, a chuckle's cast,
In this bright haven, mischief's a blast.

So grab your quills, and join the spree,
Write lines that make us smile with glee.
In this fool's abode, we won't grow old,
For every tale is a laugh retold.

Rhapsodies Beneath the Whispering Trees

Under the boughs, where shadows sneak,
A bird sings off-key, oh what a freak!
With every chirp, the sunlit glare,
I swear I saw a squirrel stare.

The leaves giggle when breezes play,
Whirling around in a merry ballet.
A raccoon flips, with a comical flair,
Grabbing a snack, like he just don't care.

In this haven of playful delight,
All the creatures seem to take flight.
As laughter echoes, loud and clear,
I raise my glass to all who cheer.

So if you wander beneath this green,
Expect the oddest sights you've seen.
In this gentle nook, the humor's grand,
Nature's jesters, all hand in hand.

Petals Fall on Ink-Stained Paths

Petals drift like thoughts untamed,
On pages inked, our lives proclaimed.
A puppy prances, chasing the breeze,
While poets fumble, with knobby knees.

As blossoms tumble, the laughter grows,
A clumsy poet steps on toes.
With every slip, and every fall,
We clutch our bellies, there's room for all.

The ink reveals our silliest fears,
Like rhyming schemes that bring us to tears.
But in this shade, we boldly write,
Of mishaps shared, our hearts alight.

So gather 'round, in this merry scene,
Where humor blooms, and jokes convene.
With every petal, a giggle's born,
In ink-stained paths, our laughter's sworn.

The Cadence of Nature's Breath

In the park, a squirrel did dance,
Chasing a breeze, oh what a prance.
A ladybug joined in the fun,
On a leaf, under the golden sun.

A beetle with swagger, he struts so bold,
While ants in a line, march, brave and cold.
The flowers giggle, they share a joke,
As a butterfly winks, in its colorful cloak.

A rabbit hops by, with quite the flair,
Tripping on daisies, without a care.
Laughter erupts from the trees all around,
In this garden of joy, where silliness is found.

So if you're stuck in a mundane grind,
Just look to the wild, and you will find,
Nature's own humor, free and diverse,
A pocket of laughter, in each universe.

Drinking in the Moonlit Lyrics

Under the night, the stars all wink,
Raccoons dance like they're on the brink.
With twinkling eyes, they plot and scheme,
Their midnight raid, a feasting dream.

The owl hoots jokes, in its own wise way,
While crickets chirp, a tuneful ballet.
A fox, with a grin, sneaks past the line,
Stealing the show—this moonlit divine!

The trees all sway, tip their leafy hats,
While badgers chill, sharing thoughts with the bats.
A firefly winks, a tiny light burst,
Lighting the laughter, quenches the thirst.

So gather your friends, let the night unfold,
Where secrets are laughed, and stories are told.
Sip the laughter like nectar so sweet,
In the glow of the moon, life is a treat.

The Sway of Melodic Leaves

Leaves rustle softly, like whispers of glee,
Dancing in rhythm, so wild and free.
A robin hops, sings an off-key tune,
While a hesitant worm wobbles, beneath the moon.

The branches shimmy, a flirty ballet,
Tickling the breeze, they laugh all day.
Grasshoppers debate, who jumps the most high,
As a bumblebee buzzes, and starts to fly.

A hedgehog rolls in, all prickly and round,
With spiky complaints about the mud on the ground.
But in the warm sun, all grumps fade away,
As critters unite in a wild cabaret.

So toss your worries to the tousled air,
Join in the fun with the creatures so rare.
In this leafy laughter, let worries all cease,
Embrace the merriment, find natural peace.

Harmonies of the Hidden Grove

In the grove, the trees sound a cheer,
With branches that sway, bringing joy near.
A frog croaks out, a comedic surprise,
While dancing pixies flutter, with mischief in their eyes.

The sun peeks through with a glittery grin,
And mushrooms chuckle, tucked under their kin.
A bear tries ballet, he trips on a vine,
While squirrels roll on, giggling divine.

The air is electric, with laughter galore,
As chipmunks tell tales that never are bore.
Each giggle, each grin, resonates in the trees,
Nature's orchestra plays, with the rustling leaves.

So slip into laughter, let the world sway,
Join the frolic in the grove, come what may.
For life's a funny story, written in light,
Let's dance with the creatures, 'neath stars shining bright.

www.ingramcontent.com/pod-product-compliance
Lightning Source LLC
Chambersburg PA
CBHW071821160426
43209CB00003B/152